# SUPERSTARS OF THE NBA FINALS

by Brendan Flynn

Cody Koala
An Imprint of Pop!
popbooksonline.com

**abdopublishing.com**
Published by Pop!, a division of ABDO, PO Box 398166, Minneapolis, Minnesota 55439. 

Printed in the United States of America, North Mankato, Minnesota

042018
092018

THIS BOOK CONTAINS RECYCLED MATERIALS

Cover Photo: Chris Szagola/AP Images
Interior Photos: Chris Szagola/AP Images, 1; Kyle Terada/Pool USA Today/AP Images, 5 (top); Wilfredo Lee/AP Images, 5 (bottom left); Shutterstock Images, 5 (bottom right); Lynne Sladky/AP Images, 6; Ron Schwane/AP Images, 9, 21; David J. Phillip/AP Images, 11; Alex Gallardo/AP Images, 12; Chuck Burton/AP Images, 15, 16; Bob Levey/AP Images, 19

Editor: Meg Gaertner
Series Designer: Laura Mitchell

**Library of Congress Control Number: 2017963433**

**Publisher's Cataloging-in-Publication Data**
Names: Flynn, Brendan, author.
Title: Superstars of the NBA finals / by Brendan Flynn.
Description: Minneapolis, Minnesota : Pop!, 2019. | Series: Sports' greatest superstars | Includes online resources and index.
Identifiers: ISBN 9781532160318 (lib.bdg.) | ISBN 9781532161438 (ebook) |
Subjects: LCSH: Basketball players--United States--Juvenile literature. | Sports records--Juvenile literature. | National Basketball Association--Juvenile literature.
Classification: DDC 796.32364--dc23

Hello! My name is

# Cody Koala

Pop open this book and you'll find QR codes like this one, loaded with information, so you can learn even more!

Scan this code* and others like it while you read, or visit the website below to make this book pop.

**popbooksonline.com/superstars-nba-finals**

*Scanning QR codes requires a web-enabled smart device with a QR code reader app and a camera.

# Table of Contents

Chapter 1

# LeBron James in the NBA Finals

The National Basketball Association (NBA) holds its finals every June. The best teams play for a chance to become **champions**.

Watch a video here!

HEAT
6
SPALDING

LeBron James played for his **hometown** team, the Cleveland Cavaliers. Later he joined the Miami Heat. James led the Heat to two NBA championship wins.

James came back to Cleveland years later. He helped the Cavaliers win their first NBA championship.

James was a star football player in high school, too.

CAVALIERS
23
CLE

Chapter 2

# Stephen Curry

Stephen Curry was a small kid. He was not very strong either. But that did not stop him from becoming one of the best players in the NBA.

Complete an activity here!

GOLDEN STATE
30
WARRIORS
WALLACE
12

Curry is a great **shooter**. He can score from almost anywhere on the court. His Golden State Warriors were NBA champions in 2015, 2017, and 2018.

Curry's father, Dell, played in the NBA for 16 seasons.

Chapter 3

# Kevin Durant

Kevin Durant joined the Warriors in 2016. They won the NBA championship the next two years.

Learn more here!

GOLDEN STATE
35
Rakuten

Durant is tall enough to score and **rebound** against big players close to the hoop. He is also quick enough to **dribble** past smaller players. He can even shoot over them far away from the basket. He is almost impossible to stop!

Chapter 4

# Kawhi Leonard

Kawhi Leonard plays for the San Antonio Spurs. He is known for his **defense**. Leonard often has to guard the best player on the other team.

Learn more here!

In 2014 the Spurs beat the Heat in the NBA Finals. Leonard successfully guarded LeBron James. Leonard was named the best player in the **series**.

**1950**

The Minneapolis Lakers win the first NBA championship.

**1966**

The Boston Celtics win their eighth NBA championship in a row.

**1998**

Michael Jordan and the Chicago Bulls win the NBA Finals for the sixth time in eight years.

**2002**

Kobe Bryant, Shaquille O'Neal, and the Los Angeles Lakers win their third straight NBA championship.

**2016**

LeBron James leads the Cavaliers to their first NBA championship.

# Making Connections

## Text-to-Self

Would you ever want to play basketball? Why or why not?

## Text-to-Text

What other great sports players have you read about? What makes them great?

## Text-to-World

What do you think makes basketball such a fun sport to watch?

# Glossary

**champion** – the best team in a sport.

**defense** – trying to stop the other team from scoring.

**dribble** – to bounce the ball, usually while moving toward the basket.

**rebound** – to grab the ball after a missed shot.

**series** – a group of games played between two teams.

**shooter** – a player who scores points by getting the ball in the basket.

# Index



## Online Resources

**popbooksonline.com**

Thanks for reading this Cody Koala book!

Scan this code* and others like it in this book, or visit the website below to make this book pop!

**popbooksonline.com/superstars-nba-finals**

*Scanning QR codes requires a web-enabled smart device with a QR code reader app and a camera.